Can You Find It?

Out in Space

A Can-You-Find-It Book

PEBBLE
a capstone imprint

Blast Off!

Can you find these things?

crayon

bananas

fish

teddy bear

snail

soda
can

tugboat

bluebird

whale

butterfly

Galaxy Delights

Can you find these things?

globe

hose

lighthouse

mermaid

mask and
snorkel

lamb

bird

gnome

poodle

tennis
racquet

Robot
Fun Run

Can you find
these things?

cheese

umbrella

iron

bow

spray
bottle

 fork

 hot dog

 bee

 wizard
hat

pencil

Walking on the Moon

Can you find these things?

sea horse

gumball machine

pitcher

trumpet

birdcage

mouse

strawberry

crown

pretzel

apple

Make a Wish!

Can you find these things?

baseball

jet

polar bear

elephant

daisy

toilet paper

dragon

dust pan

robot

bride

Big Star, Little Stars

Can you find these things?

 Saturn

 avocado

 taco

 koala

tissue box

school bus

pear

xylophone

deer

cupid

An Alien Welcome

Can you find these things?

guitar

candle

watering can

Pegasus

heart

 starfish

 mushroom

 tulip

 olive

 ice-cream cone

Star Pictures

Can you find these things?

ship

zebra

piano

soccer ball

tent

 ice skate

 killer whale

 saw

 motorcycle

 skull

So Many Satellites!

Can you find these things?

 toucan

 lion

 horse

 seal

hat

 mitten

 saxophone

 scissors

 owl

 police car

Playful Planets

Can you find these things?

ant

dolphin

hot-air balloon

comb

astronaut

ladybug

alien

sunflower

plum

witch's
shoe

Looking at the Sky

Can you find these things?

egg

rose

yarn

fire
hydrant

doghouse

purse

lobster

dragonfly

cap

cactus

Marvelous Mars

Can you find
these things?

tiger

bike

corn

raccoon

anchor

jack-o'-
lantern

chef's
hat

fish
bones

snowman

spider

Lunar Eclipse

Can you find
these things?

sewing
machine

record

horseshoe

grill

peach

TV

eagle

clothespin

billiard ball

mixer

Space Camp

Can you find these things?

fishbowl

ghost

golf ball

cake

bunny

 brush

 llama

 bowling pin

 nurse

 cowboy

Psst! Did you know that Pebs the Pebble was hiding
in EVERY PUZZLE in this book?

It's true! Go back and look!

Hi.

Look for other books in this series:

I would like to dedicate this book to my amazing and supportive family and friends—with a very special thank you to Heidi Thompson, my boss and my friend. Never thought that work could be so much fun. — KD

Pebble Sprout is published by Pebble, an imprint of Capstone.
1710 Roe Crest Drive, North Mankato, Minnesota 56003
www.capstonepub.com

Library of Congress Cataloging-in-Publication Data

Names: Dubke, Karon, author.
Title: Out in space : a can-you-find-it book / Karon Dubke.
Description: North Mankato : Capstone Press, [2021] | Series: Can you find it? | Audience: Ages 6-8 | Audience: Grades K-1 | Summary: "Send kids on an out-of-this-world seek-and-find adventure. Planets, moons, shooting stars, and countless other celestial objects make finding the hidden items in the full-color photo puzzles a blast. Pictographs and word labels are included in each to-find list"— Provided by publisher.
Identifiers: LCCN 2020030970 (print) | LCCN 2020030971 (ebook) | ISBN 9781977132130 (hardcover) | ISBN 9781977133151 (paperback) | ISBN 9781977154712 (ebook)
Subjects: LCSH: Outer space—Juvenile literature. | Outer space—Exploration—Juvenile literature.
Classification: LCC QB500.22 .D83 2021 (print) | LCC QB500.22 (ebook) | DDC 523—dc23
LC record available at https://lccn.loc.gov/2020030970
LC ebook record available at https://lccn.loc.gov/2020030971

Image Credits: All photos by Capstone Studio/Karon Dubke

Editorial Credits: Jill Kalz, editor; Heidi Thompson, designer; Karon Dubke, set stylist; Kathy McColley, production specialist